TRUMPET FOR KIDS

TRUMPET FOR KIDS

Christmas Carols, Classical Music, Nursery Rhymes, Traditional & Folk Songs!

TRUMPET FOR KIDS:

Christmas Carols, Classical Music, Nursery Rhymes, Traditional & Folk Songs!

© JAVIER MARCÓ

ISBN-13:978-1499243512
ISBN-10:1499243510

Contents

Playing guide

Standard notation
Notes are written on a Staff.

Staff
The staff consists of five lines and four spaces, on which notes symbols are placed.

Clef
A clef assigns an individual note to a certain line. The **Treble Clef** or **G Clef** is used for the trumpet.

This clef indicates the position of the note G which is on the second line from the bottom.

Note
A note is a sign used to represent the relative pitch of a sound. There are seven notes: A, B, C, D, E, F and G.

Ledger lines
The ledger lines are used to inscribe notes outside the lines and spaces of the staff.

Accidentals
An accidental is a symbol to raise or lower the pitch of a note.

♯ sharp	Next note up half step.
♭ flat	Next note down half step.
♮ natural	Cancels a flat or a sharp.

Note values

A **note value** is used to indicate the duration of a note. A **rest** is an interval of silence, marked by a sign indicating the length of the pause. Each rest corresponds to a particular note value.

○	Whole note	▬	Whole rest
♩	Half note	▬	Half rest
♩	Quarter note	𝄽	Quarter rest
♪	Eight note	𝄾	Eight rest
♬	Sixteenth note	𝄿	Sixteenth rest

Dotted note

A dotted note is a note with a small dot written after it. The dot adds half as much again to the basic note's duration.

Tie

A tie is a curved line connecting the heads of two notes of the same pitch, indicating that they are to be played as a single note with a duration equal to the sum of the individual notes' note values.

Bars or Measures

The staff is divided into equal segments of time consisting of the same number of beats, called bar or measures.

Measure   Measure   Measure   Measure

↑

Bar line

Time signature

Time signature consists of two numbers, the upper number specifies how many beats (or counts) are in each measure, and the lower number tells us the note value which represents one beat.

one   two   three   four

Example: 4/4 means four quarters, or four beats per measure with a quarter note receiving one beat or count.

Key signature

A Key signature is a group of accidentals, generally written at the beginning of a score immediately after the clef, and shows which notes always get sharps or flats. Accidentals on the lines and spaces in the key signature affect those notes throughout the piece unless there is a natural sign.

First and second endings

The section should be repeated from the beginning, and number brackets above the bars indicate which to played the first time (1), which to play the second time (2).

Dynamics

Dynamics refers to the volume of the notes.

p   (piano), meaning soft.
mp   (mezzo-piano), meaning "moderately soft".
mf   (mezzo-forte), meaning "moderately loud".
f   (forte), meaning loud.

Crescendo. A gradual increase in volume.

Decrescendo. A gradual decrease in volume.

Tempo Markings

Tempo is written at the beginning of a piece of music and indicates how slow or fast this piece should be played.

Adagio — slow and stately (66–76 bpm)

Andate — at a walking pace (76–108 bpm)

Moderato — moderately (101-110 bpm)

Allegro — fast, quickly and bright (120–139 bpm)

Allegretto — moderately fast (but less so than allegro)

Presto — extremely fast (180–200 bpm)

Articulation

Legato. Notes are played smoothly and connected.

Stacatto. Notes are played separated or detached from its neighbours by a silence.

Fermata (pause)
The note is to be prolonged at the pleasure of the performer.

Aloutte

Traditionnel

Amazing Grace

Traditional

Andante

mf

America The Beautiful

Samuel A. Ward

Moderato

Arroz Con Leche

Tradicional

Allegro

Aserrín, Aserrán

Tradicional

Allegro

Aura Lee

George R. Poulton

Cielito Lindo

Quirino Mendoza y Cortés

For He's a Jolly Good Fellow

Traditional

Allegro

Frere Jacques

Traditionnel

Go Tell Aunt Rhody

Traditional

Good Morning To All

Patty & Mildred J. Hill

Allegro

Greensleves

Traditional

Andante

mf

Jingle Bells

James Lord Pierpont

La Cucaracha

Tradicional

La Donna è Mobile

Giuseppe Verdi

Las Mañanitas

Tradicional

Allegro

London Bridge Is Falling Down

Traditional

Allegro

Mary Had A Little Lamb

Traditional

Presto

mf

Menuett

Johann Sebastian Bach

Allegretto

My Bonnie Lies Over The Ocean

Traditional

Ode an die Freude

Ludwig Van Beethoven

Moderato

Oh! Susanna

Stephen Foster

Old MacDonald Had A Farm

Traditional

Presto

mf

Row Row Row Your Boat

Traditional

Scarborough Fair

Traditional

Allegro

mp

Stille Nacht, heilige Nacht

Franz Xaver Gruber

Sur le Pont d'Avignon

Traditionnel

Allegro

The House Of The Rising Sun

Traditional

Moderato

The Star-Spangled Banner

Music by John Stafford Smith

Moderato

Twinkle Twinkle Little Star

W. A. Mozart

Un Elefante Se Balanceaba

Tradicional

Allegro

We Wish You A Merry Christmas

Traditional

Presto

mf

When Johnny Comes Marching Home

Traditional

Allegro

mf

When The Saints Go Marching In

Traditional

Presto

Wiegenlied

Johannes Brahms

Adagio

mp

Yankee Doodle

Traditional

Allegro

info@marcomusica.com

ʋ

58215495R00030

Made in the USA
Lexington, KY
06 December 2016